QUESTIONING HISTORY

Nazi Germany

Alex Woolf

HODDER
Wayland

an imprint of Hodder Children's Books

© 2004 White-Thomson Publishing Ltd

Produced for Hodder Wayland by
White-Thomson Publishing Ltd
2/3 St Andrew's Place
Lewes BN7 1UP

Editor: Kelly Davis
Designer: Angie Allison
Consultant: Michael Rawcliffe
Picture researcher: Kelly Davis
Proofreader: David C. Sills, Proof Positive
Reading Service

Published in Great Britain in 2004 by Hodder
Wayland, an imprint of Hodder Children's Books

British Library Cataloguing in Publication Data
Woolf, Alex
   Nazi Germany - (Questioning History)
   1. Germany - History - 1933-1945 - Juvenile
   literature I. Title
   943'.086
ISBN 0 7502 4514 X

Printed by C&C Offset Printing Co., Ltd, China

Hodder Children's Books
A division of Hodder Headline Limited
338 Euston Road, London NW1 3BH

Picture acknowledgements:

akg-images, London 5, 6, 38; Hodder Wayland
Picture Library 13, 15, 19, 22 and 60, 23 and *title
page*, 24 and 60, 27, 31, 37 and 61, 43, 44, 46, 54,
56, 57 and 61; Popperfoto 4, 9, 12, 18, 29, 33, 34,
35, 36, 40, 42, 45, 48, 49, 50, 51, 52, 53, 55, 58;
M. Rawcliffe 7, 8, 10 and *cover*, 16, 20, 21, 26, 28,
30, 32.

The maps on pages 25 and 41 were produced by
The Map Studio.

Cover picture: Hitler being saluted by the crowd as
he arrives at the 1929 Nuremberg rally.

CONTENTS

CHAPTER 1

The Rise of the Nazis, 1918–33

In 1933, the Nazi Party, an extreme nationalist and racist organization, came to power in Germany. They ruled with an iron fist, persecuting ethnic minorities, especially the Jews, and leading the country into a disastrous war, causing millions of deaths. How did the German people allow the Nazis to take over their country and cause so much suffering? To answer this question, it is necessary to look at the history of Germany in the century leading up to the Nazi takeover.

THE ROOTS OF NATIONAL SOCIALISM

The German nation came into being in 1871 when Prussia, the largest kingdom in a group of independent Germanic states, conquered the others to form one country. Prussian political ideas, including a respect for authority and an aggressive foreign policy, dominated the new nation. This made it easier for an extremist group like the Nazis to take power.

During the nineteenth century, many Germans became influenced by nationalist and racist ideas. Writers such as Joseph Gobineau claimed that the German people had been weakened by intermarrying with other ethnic groups. This conservative, racist, *völkisch* (literally 'folkish') ideology lay behind what became national socialism, or Nazism.

BELOW *Johann Fichte, a nineteenth-century German nationalist, who emphasized the heroism of the German race and helped to lay the foundations of national socialism.*

THE FIRST WORLD WAR

In 1914, Germany (with Austria-Hungary and ~~Italy~~) went to war

WRONG!

against Russia, France and Britain, causing an upsurge of nation-alist feeling. However, the war led to food shortages, inflation, and worsening living conditions for many Germans. The Nazi Party later exploited these grievances.

ABOVE *An armed uprising in Berlin in 1919. Many middle-class Germans feared their country was on the verge of a revolution.*

? EVENT IN QUESTION

Did the Treaty of Versailles help the rise of the Nazis?

After they won the First World War, the victorious allies forced Germany to sign a peace treaty at Versailles in 1919. Many Germans felt that their country had been betrayed by its leaders. Under the treaty, Germany had to give up parts of its territory, substantially reduce its army and navy, and agree not to rearm. In addition, Germany had to pay large sums of money, known as reparations, to the victorious powers to compensate for the damage caused by the war. The treaty created a mood of national humiliation and betrayal, which made it easier for the Nazis, who promised national revival, to gain support. However, some historians downplay the importance of Versailles in the rise of the Nazis. They argue that Germany was already an unstable country, on the brink of dictatorship, before 1919, because its constitution (written in 1871) tended to give too much power to extremist groups.

ABOVE *The young Hitler (front row, far left) with fellow soldiers during the First World War. Hitler proved to be a brave and dutiful soldier, though he was never promoted beyond the rank of corporal.*

THE WEIMAR REPUBLIC

In November 1918, following Germany's defeat, strikes and protests erupted across the country. The government and the emperor were overthrown, and replaced by a new government under Friedrich Ebert, leader of the Socialist Party (SPD). During this chaotic period, many richer Germans, as well as those from the lower middle classes, feared there would be a communist revolution, like the one that had occurred in Russia in November 1917 under Lenin.

To calm these fears, Germany's political parties framed a new constitution, intended to give the people more power. Germany became the Weimar Republic (named after the town where the parties met), with an elected president and a more powerful parliament.

THE BIRTH OF THE NAZI PARTY

In spite of these reforms, the growing fear of communism led to the establishment of right-wing *völkisch* parties throughout the

Adolf Hitler (1889–1945)

Hitler was born in Braunau, Austria, the son of a customs official. Historians have long debated how a man of such humble origins – and not even a German citizen – could come to dominate Germany. As the historian Alan Bullock has pointed out, Hitler was actually quite lazy and easily bored by administrative work. What he did have was *'political genius'*, according to Gordon Craig. He had a great sense of timing, always knowing when his enemies were at their most vulnerable, and possessed an unshakeable belief in himself as a man of destiny. However, other historians, such as A.J.P. Taylor, have claimed that Hitler's rise was more to do with luck than skill. He was simply in the right place, at the right time. Taylor argues that German history, leading to the Second World War, would probably have followed a similar course, with or without Hitler.

BELOW *Hitler was a highly effective public speaker, making great use of gestures and poses which he used to practise beforehand in front of a mirror.*

country. One of these, based in Bavaria, in southern Germany, was the German Workers' Party (DAP). In February 1920, the DAP changed its name to the German National Socialist Workers' Party (NSDAP), or Nazi Party.

In 1919, an ex-army corporal called Adolf Hitler had joined the then DAP and soon gained a following. Hitler inspired fanatical loyalty. He was not an original thinker, but he had a genius for public speaking. He was able to express the anger, fear and bitterness felt by many Germans about what was happening to their country. Before long, Hitler joined the party's committee. Then, after a power struggle with the party's original members, he became leader in July 1921.

THE PARTY GROWS

Anti-semitism (prejudice against Jews) was quite common in the 1920s, particularly among the *völkisch* parties. In times of hardship, people often look for someone to blame for their troubles, and the Jews, with their different culture and traditions, were an easy target. In his speeches, Hitler blamed Germany's defeat on the Jews and the communists.

Under Hitler's leadership, the party became a highly organized, disciplined force. It adopted a symbol, the swastika, which was displayed on banners and armbands. In August 1921 the Nazis formed a private army called the *Sturmabteilung* (SA). By 1923, the SA had 55,000 members.

BELOW *During the period of hyper-inflation in 1923, high-value banknotes were specially printed, including a 50-million mark note shown here. Despite their large face value, these notes quickly became worthless.*

THE BEERHALL COUP

Meanwhile, the burden of war debts was taking a severe toll on the German economy and unemployment was rising. Then, in autumn 1923, Germany suffered 'hyper-inflation', when the currency lost almost all its value.

The state government in Bavaria, where the Nazis were based, was particularly hostile to the national government. Hitler used this situation to make a bid for power. In November, he and his comrades seized the Bavarian government leaders in a beerhall in Munich, and then tried to persuade them to join in an uprising against the national government. The coup failed when the Bavarian politicians escaped, and the state police and army stayed

loyal. The following day, the Nazis tried to continue the coup by marching into the centre of Munich but they were easily defeated by the police. Hitler, who was slightly injured, fled the scene, and was arrested two days later.

ABOVE *A defiant-looking Hitler about to face trial for his part in the Beerhall Coup. On Hitler's right stands Erich von Ludendorff, a famous First World War general, and a key figure in the coup.*

? WHAT IF…

Hitler had died during the Beerhall Coup?

As 2,000 Nazis marched towards Odeon Square in the centre of Munich on 9 November, they were confronted by armed police. Shots were fired, and Hitler was pulled to the ground by a comrade, who was fatally wounded by a bullet. Another Nazi, Ulrich Graf, threw himself over the party leader, almost certainly saving his life. Graf was then killed, hit by eleven bullets. But what would have happened if Graf had not saved Hitler that day? Without Hitler's forceful personality and single-minded ambition, would the Nazi Party have been able to survive and rebuild itself after the wilderness years of the mid-1920s? Even during Hitler's brief absence in prison, the party began to collapse. Popular support for national socialism would probably have revived during the crisis years of the early 1930s, but without Hitler it is difficult to see how the Nazis could have actually taken power.

HITLER GOES TO PRISON

At his trial, Hitler claimed that he had acted as a patriot, trying to overthrow the traitors who had signed the Treaty of Versailles. The court was impressed and gave him the minimum sentence of five years. In the end, he only served thirteen months in prison.

REBUILDING THE PARTY

On his release, in December 1924, Hitler found the Nazi Party weak and divided. With the economy improving, there was less support for extreme right-wing movements like the Nazis. Undaunted, Hitler set about reorganizing the party, setting up local branches all over the country. The party's new strategy was not to seize power, but to obtain it legally by winning seats in the Reichstag (the German parliament). The Nazis fought their first election in May 1928 and won just 2.6 per cent of the vote.

BELOW *From 1927, the Nazis began holding annual mass rallies in the ancient city of Nuremberg. Each year these stage-managed occasions became larger and more theatrical. Here, Hitler is saluted by the crowd as he arrives at the 1929 rally.*

DEPRESSION

In 1930 the German economy again lurched into crisis. By September 1930, there were 3 million unemployed, and by 1932 this had risen to 6 million. This was good news for the Nazis, who exploited the people's misery in order to win support. The Weimar Republic became a major target for their criticism. They argued that Germany's attempt at parliamentary democracy had failed to solve the country's economic problems.

In contrast to the weak, divided government, the Nazis appeared well-organized and united behind a strong leader. While continuing to proclaim their rejection of the Treaty of Versailles and their plans to revive German national pride, the Nazis were careful to avoid spelling out their policies, for fear of alienating sections of the population that disagreed with them.

? EVENT IN QUESTION

What does Mein Kampf *tell us about* Hitler?

Hitler spent much of his time in prison writing a book called *Mein Kampf* ('My Struggle'). In it he poured out his hatred of Jews and communists, who he believed to be conspiring together to take over the world. He argued that the German race (which he called the Aryan race) was superior to all others. And he believed that Aryan supremacy was being threatened by intermarriage, particularly with Jews. He also talked about his dreams of making Germany powerful again by expanding the country to the east. Some have argued that the book's themes of anti-semitism and military conquest prove that Hitler planned the Holocaust and the invasion of the Soviet Union all along. However, most historians agree that *Mein Kampf* sets out Hitler's basic beliefs rather than his definite plans. Hitler took advantage of opportunities that arose later to put these principles into practice.

11

ELECTION SUCCESS

The Nazis broadened their appeal, attracting support from small businessmen, farmers, wealthy conservatives, students and older Germans. In the election of September 1930, they won an astonishing 6.5 million votes, giving them a total of 107 seats in the 600-seat Reichstag.

As the economy worsened during 1931–2, the Nazis became even more popular. In April 1932, Hitler stood for election for German president. He lost to the retired general, Paul von Hindenburg, but nevertheless won 12 million votes. After elections in July 1932, the Nazis became the largest party in the Reichstag, with 230 seats. This was just short of an overall majority, but Hindenburg, who disliked Hitler, refused to offer him the post of chancellor (the chief minister of government). Instead, the job went to Franz von Papen of the conservative Centre Party.

BELOW *By 1930, Hitler was rapidly achieving celebrity status. Here, crowds surround his car, showering him with flowers.*

HITLER BECOMES CHANCELLOR

This was a difficult period for the Nazis. Their public image was damaged by the increasingly violent actions of their brown-shirted street army, the SA, in its clashes with communist supporters. The Nazi vote declined in a further set of elections in November 1932. But, despite these set-backs, events were moving in their favour. Von Papen, who lacked popular support, resigned in December, and his successor, General von Schleicher, was equally unsuccessful. Von Papen then persuaded Hindenburg to appoint Hitler chancellor, and himself vice-chancellor. His plan was to try to control Hitler and his party by bringing the Nazi leader into government. Hindenburg reluctantly agreed, and on 30 January 1933 Hitler became chancellor.

DER MARSCHALL UND DER GEFREITE

KÄMPFEN MIT UNS FÜR FRIEDEN UND GLEICHBERECHTIGUNG

ABOVE *An election poster from 1933, showing Hitler with Paul von Hindenburg.*

? EVENT IN QUESTION

Who voted for the Nazis?

In 1928, just 2.6 per cent of the electorate voted for the Nazis. This increased to 37.3 per cent in 1932. Where had all these extra votes come from? Historians used to assume that most Nazi voters were rural Germans or lower middle-class city-dwellers (such as small businessmen or office workers), because these groups were the main targets of Nazi propaganda, which played on their fears of big business, trade unions and communism. However, the Nazis actually gained support from many other groups as well, such as the upper middle classes and manual workers. Another misconception held by post-war historians was that the typical Nazi voter was young and male. In fact, in July 1932, more women voted for the Nazis. The elderly were also attracted to the Nazis, especially those whose savings had gone down in value because of inflation. The truth is that the Nazis attracted support from almost every group in German society.

13

CHAPTER 2

The Nazis Take Power, 1933–34

As leader of the largest party in the Reichstag, Hitler was in a very strong position. In February, he won over the leaders of the German army by promising that the military would be expanded – in defiance of the Treaty of Versailles. He then increased his power by giving government jobs to leading Nazi Party members. He made his long-term ally, Hermann Goering, Minister of the Interior in Prussia, placing him in charge of the largest police force in Germany. Another senior colleague, Joseph Goebbels, was made Minister of Propaganda.

THE REICHSTAG FIRE

On 27 February 1933, the Reichstag building burned down, and a communist confessed to having started the fire. The following day, an emergency decree was signed, giving the government the power to control public meetings and newspapers, and arrest anyone they wanted. Communists were declared enemies of the state, and the SA was given the freedom to attack them in the streets.

However, despite their growing power, and their control of state radio, the Nazis only won 288 seats in the election on 5 March. To form a majority in the Reichstag, they still needed the support of the Nationalist Party, with 52 seats.

THE ENABLING LAW

On 23 March, the Reichstag met to discuss the Enabling Bill. This proposed to extend the 'state of emergency' for another four years, giving the government the power to pass laws without consulting the Reichstag. Because this was a constitutional change, Hitler required a two-thirds majority. Through a mixture of threats and promises, he obtained the required number of votes from the other parties. The passing of the Enabling Law signalled the end of parliamentary democracy in Germany.

Who burned down the Reichstag?

On 27 February, a student passing by the Reichstag saw through the first-floor windows a man carrying a burning torch. Ten minutes later, smoke and flames were pouring from the building. Soon, only the walls remained standing. A dazed, half-naked Dutchman, Marinus van der Lubbe, was found at the scene. Because of his communist connections, Nazi leaders used the event as an excuse to take decisive action against the communists. Van der Lubbe was executed. However, there is little evidence to link him to the crime, especially as it was later found that he was three-quarters blind. Subsequent investigations have suggested that the most likely culprits were an SA group headed by Nazi leader Reinhard Heydrich.

LEFT *The Reichstag in flames. When Hitler heard about the fire he gave orders that the Communist Party leaders be hanged that very night. Hindenburg rejected this but agreed that Hitler should receive emergency powers.*

15

ABOVE *Hitler with
President Paul von
Hindenburg in May
1933. The president
was so popular that
Hitler could not take
full power until
Hindenburg's death
in 1934.*

THE NAZI REVOLUTION

Over the next twelve months, the Nazis abolished or took control of almost every institution that might threaten their position as masters of Germany. In May 1933, the trade unions were replaced with the Nazi-controlled German Labour Front, and all rival political parties were forced to close down. By early 1934, the state governments (such as Bavaria) were abolished, and the whole country was ruled from Berlin.

While the Nazi leadership tightened its grip on the country's institutions, the brutality of the SA continued. With the law now on their side, SA members beat up Jews and communists and destroyed trade union offices. In April, Goebbels organized a boycott of all Jewish-owned shops.

THE PURGE OF THE SA

Hitler believed that he had to work with big business, the civil service and the army in order to keep the country going and build

? **WHAT IF...**

Hitler had not moved against Roehm?

In early 1934, conservative figures such as von Papen were beginning to regret having brought Hitler to power. Some even talked of overthrowing him and restoring the monarchy. Hitler was certainly vulnerable at this point. He knew that destroying the SA would reassure the establishment and the army, and secure his position, yet he hesitated to confront Roehm. If he had not been persuaded by the other Nazi Party leaders that this was a necessary step, it is likely that Hitler would eventually have been overthrown, either by Roehm, or by a conservative alliance backed by the army.

his new regime. However, the SA became impatient. They wanted to take the Nazi revolution even further by destroying big business, allowing the party to run the state, and giving the SA control of the army.

The SA leader, Ernst Roehm, with over 2.5 million men at his command, was the only man with the power to threaten Hitler. By the end of 1933, the street violence of the SA was becoming an embarrassment to Hitler, undermining his support among senior figures in the military, the civil service and industry. A confrontation between the two men had become almost inevitable.

After much hesitation, Hitler finally acted on 30 June 1934. In what became known as 'the Night of the Long Knives', around 85 of the SA leaders, including Roehm, were arrested and shot. Thereafter, the SA ceased to pose a threat. When President Hindenburg died in August 1934, Hitler combined the positions of president and chancellor to become absolute ruler of Germany.

CHAPTER 3

The Police State

Despite appearances, Nazi Germany was not run particularly efficiently. The three main centres of power were Hitler himself, the Reich ministries, and the Nazi Party. These power centres competed for influence, often creating confusion at the heart of government, which Hitler did little to resolve.

THE ROLE OF HITLER

As Führer (leader) of the country, the party and the military, Hitler was undoubtedly the most powerful person in Nazi Germany. Yet he was quite a remote leader, preferring to hand over the day-to-day running of the country to his subordinates. He rarely gave direct orders, and ministers were often forced to interpret his vague statements for themselves when deciding on policies.

BELOW *Hitler spent much of his time far from the Reichstag – at the Berghof, his retreat in the Bavarian mountains. Here, he is seen relaxing with his mistress Eva Braun and his dogs.*

Heinrich Himmler (1900–1945)

As head of the *Schutzstaffel* (SS), the powerful secret
police force, Himmler was responsible for Germany's
concentration camps, where political prisoners were
routinely tortured and murdered. Under his leadership,
the SS carried out the mass killings of Jews in the east,
and he was a key figure in organizing the Holocaust.
Experts have long puzzled over how a man such as
Himmler, who came from an ordinary middle-class
family, could have behaved so monstrously as an adult.
The historian Gerald Reitlinger says there was nothing
in Himmler's childhood to explain his later actions. But
Klaus Fischer, an expert on the Nazis, disagrees. He
points out that Himmler's father was extremely strict
and the young Himmler was lonely and insecure. He
had no real sense of his own identity until he joined the
Nazi Party. From then on, he attached himself
completely to Hitler and national socialism. For him, the
Nazis' racist view of the world became almost a religion. This, Fischer
claims, helps to explain his later fanaticism.

ABOVE *Heinrich
Himmler, was one
of the most feared
personalities in Nazi
Germany. His goal was
to use terror to build a
'racially pure' nation.*

REICH MINISTRIES

There were sixteen Reich ministers, each controlling a different
department of state. At first, these ministers were able to exercise
considerable influence through meetings of the cabinet.
However, after 1933, Hitler preferred dealing with them one-to-
one, and the cabinet met much less frequently. The most powerful
ministers, such as Joseph Goebbels and Wilhelm Frick, were the
ones responsible for fulfilling Hitler's grand plans for German
expansion and racial purification.

THE PARTY

In 1933, the Nazi Party's main function was to produce propaganda on behalf of the government, and to ensure that the will of
the Führer was carried out by the departments of state. However,
its influence remained weak until 1938 when it experienced a
revival (see page 45).

ECONOMIC RECOVERY

When the Nazis came to power, the government was virtually bankrupt, unemployment was well over 6 million, and industrial production had declined dramatically. The Nazis tried to boost the economy by investing in a number of public schemes, such as the *Autobahn* project to build 7,000 km (4,350 miles) of motorways across the country. The introduction of military conscription in 1935 also helped to create jobs, ensuring that each year a million young men were given employment for two years.

BELOW *A German postcard, sent in 1936, showing Hitler helping to lay the foundations of the* Autobahn *in 1933, next to a view of one of the new motorways.*

23.9.1933 Erſter Spatenſtich
23.9.1936 1000 km Autobahn fertig

As the economy revived, the government kept inflation down by keeping wages and prices firmly under control. Business confidence was promoted by government subsidies (grants of money) for house construction, and tax reductions to help the motor industry. As a result of all these efforts, unemployment had fallen to 1.7 million by autumn 1935.

REARMAMENT AND THE FOUR-YEAR PLAN

Hitler's overriding ambition was to rearm Germany as quickly as possible. However, the reviving economy had led to a steep rise in imports. As a result, a lot of currency was flowing out of the country, leaving insufficient money to pay for the raw materials needed for rearmament.

To solve this problem, in 1936 Hitler introduced the Four-Year Plan, aiming to make Germany less dependent on imports by increasing industrial and agricultural production. In four years' time, the German economy and army would be ready for war. In fact, the Four-Year Plan failed to achieve its targets – mainly because of inefficiencies in its administration – but it did provide money for rearmament.

BELOW *A carefully posed portrait of Hermann Goering, wearing the medals he won for his flying exploits in the First World War.*

? PEOPLE IN QUESTION

Hermann Goering (1893–1946)

Goering, an ace pilot in the First World War, had great strengths as a senior Nazi henchman. Generous, friendly, intelligent and daring, he was one of the few Nazi leaders who was genuinely popular with the German people. But he could also be vain, greedy and appallingly cruel. Did Goering ultimately prove a help or a hindrance to the Nazi cause? As head of the *Luftwaffe* (the German air force), his energy and popularity were great assets. However, his weaknesses became clear when Hitler placed him in charge of the Four-Year Plan. Goering tried to expand his powers and take complete control of Germany's economy. This led to clashes with existing ministries, inefficiencies and rivalries that undermined the success of the plan. Later, Goering's celebrated *Luftwaffe* failed to defeat the RAF in the Battle of Britain or prevent the bombing of Germany, and he ended the war in disgrace.

Baut
Jugendherbergen und Heime

PROPAGANDA

The Nazis used all available media – radio, newspapers, films, theatre and books – to win over the German people to the idea of national socialism. The department responsible for this task was the newly created Ministry of Public Enlightenment and Propaganda, headed by Joseph Goebbels.

RADIO AND NEWSPAPERS

Millions of cheap radios were produced, and local radio wardens were appointed to encourage people to buy them, so they could hear Nazi propaganda in their homes. Local and national radio stations came under the control of the Reich Radio Company, which only broadcast programmes approved by the ministry.

ABOVE *Posters were a vital propaganda tool for the Nazis. In this one, a pretty young girl asks the German people to give money to help 'Build Youth Hostels and Homes'. In reality, all the money collected was used to pay for armaments.*

All left-wing newspapers were closed down in early 1933, and the remaining newspapers were taken over by the Reich Press Chamber. The editors of these papers were obliged to print the views of the regime.

THE ARTS

The Propaganda Ministry laid down strict rules for theatre, film, art, music and literature. For example, books that glorified war or German heroism were encouraged, while anti-war books were banned. In art, modern or experimental forms, such as the works of the Dutch impressionist Van Gogh, were condemned as 'degenerate'. Hitler, a failed artist himself, favoured sentimental country scenes showing peasants working in the fields, or battle scenes with warriors in heroic poses.

Joseph Goebbels (1897–1945)

Goebbels is remembered in history as the Nazis' most brilliant 'spin doctor'. But how successful was he in reality? Goebbels was a jealous, insecure man, and he spent a lot of time fighting bitter battles with his colleagues for control over areas which he considered part of his responsibility. He fought with Rosenberg over culture, Goering over art, Bouhler over literature, and Ribbentrop over propaganda in the occupied countries. The truth was that Goebbels' status within the Nazi leadership steadily declined during the 1930s as different departments took on propagandist roles. As organizer of *Kristallnacht* (see page 36), a nationwide attack on Jewish synagogues and businesses in 1938, he was briefly popular again. But the international outrage that followed this event weakened his position further.

FOREIGN POLICY

Hitler's immediate priorities were to destroy the Versailles Treaty, rearm, and seek alliances with other countries. Only when these aims had been achieved would he feel strong enough to confront France, Germany's hostile neighbour. Once France had been dealt with, he would be free to pursue his ambitions to create *Lebensraum* ('living space') for the German people in Russia.

BELOW *The Nazis also made a number of propaganda films, most famously* Triumph of the Will *about the 1934 Nuremberg rally. The scenes of marching columns, swirling banners and vast audiences listening spellbound to Hitler's speeches, conveyed the sense of an unstoppable mass movement. Here, Hitler reviews the 1935 Nuremberg rally.*

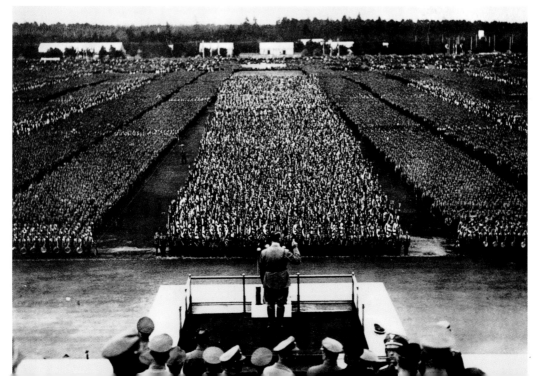

GERMAN AGGRESSION

By 1935, the German army had trebled in size, and weapons production had been increased – in defiance of the Treaty of Versailles. In March 1936, Hitler sent German troops into the Rhineland, an area between France and Germany that had been controlled by the French and British under the Versailles Treaty. By November 1937, Hitler had signed agreements with Italy and Japan, ending Germany's diplomatic isolation.

Austria was mainly populated by ethnic Germans who wanted Austria to become part of Germany. Hitler – as an Austrian and a believer in a greater Germany – also desired this, but the *Anschluss* (union) of Germany and Austria was forbidden by the Treaty of Versailles. By February 1938, Hitler felt strong enough to ignore the treaty, and he sent a German force to Austria. There was no resistance, and Austria was absorbed into the Reich.

Ethnic Germans living in the Sudetenland region of Czechoslovakia also wished to become part of Germany. Despite French and British efforts to dissuade him, Hitler sent his troops into Sudetenland in October 1938. By March 1939, the whole country, including the regions of Bohemia, Moravia and Slovakia, was under German control.

BELOW *German troops march into the Rhineland in 1936. Hitler later described the event as the most nerve-racking of his life. If the French had responded, 'we would have been forced to withdraw with our tails between our legs' he said.*

Germany
Rhineland, remilitarized 1936
International boundary, 1937
Austria, unified with Germany, March 1938
Sudetenland, annexed by Germany, September 1938
Bohemia, Moravia and Slovakia under German control by March 1939

ABOVE *A map showing the extent of German expansion by March 1939.*

THE OUTBREAK OF WAR

Hitler's next objective was Poland, which occupied lands taken from Germany by the Treaty of Versailles. The British and French warned Germany that they would declare war if any more countries were invaded, but Hitler surprised them by signing a non-aggression pact with the Soviet Union (securing his eastern border in the event of a war in Western Europe). Then, on 1 September, the German Army invaded Poland. On 3 September, Britain and France declared war on Germany. The Second World War had begun.

? WHAT IF...

the French had driven Germany out of the Rhineland?

In 1936, Britain and France were still militarily stronger than Germany. Hitler sent a small force of just 22,000 men, and if the French had decided to intervene he would have been forced to withdraw. The French were horrified by Hitler's invasion, but were unwilling to take action without the support of the British, who were not prepared to go to war over the issue. Had France acted decisively at this stage, it could have shown that German expansion would not be tolerated, and Hitler might have been stopped in his tracks. War would probably not have occurred in 1939, although it may have broken out later, since the same tensions would have continued to exist in Europe.

CHAPTER 4

Life in Nazi Germany, 1933–39

Goebbels once said that in Nazi Germany, 'no German felt himself to be a private citizen'. By encouraging Germans to think of the state before themselves, the Nazis hoped to gain complete control over the population.

ABOVE *A mass rally at night in the early 1930s. 'At such meetings,' Goebbels commented, 'the individual changes from a little worm into part of a large dragon.'*

SOCIETY AND CULTURE

There were frequent marches, parades and other large-scale activities designed to create a sense of national pride and group identity. The most famous examples were the mass rallies, often held at night. Searchlights would illuminate the sky, producing the sense of being in a giant cathedral. Indeed, many compared these events to religious experiences. The regime also filled the calendar

? EVENT IN QUESTION

How did the Reich Cultural Chamber affect German culture?

In September 1933, the Reich Cultural Chamber (RCC) was set up, to prevent German writers, artists, film-makers and musicians from producing work that the Nazis disapproved of. All creative Germans were forced to join this organization, and many decided to leave Germany in protest. However, many other artists and intellectuals stayed, joined the RCC and continued their work. Some may have genuinely believed that their art would not be interfered with, while others could not resist the public acclaim given to them by the regime. The RCC did not always ban the work of those they disapproved of. For instance, in 1937, there was an exhibition entitled 'Degenerate Art' in Munich, which visitors were invited to mock. The composer Richard Strauss was able to continue working, and even to collaborate with a Jewish writer, but only because of his international reputation. So it seems that German culture was severely weakened under the Nazis, but it did continue.

ABOVE On 10 May 1933, the German Student Union staged an event called 'the burning of the books' destroying a large number of 'un-German', foreign and Jewish books. This was an example of the way the Nazis used German patriotism to destroy the things they disapproved of.

with holidays and commemorations. Important dates included 30 January, the day Hitler was appointed chancellor; 24 February, the founding of the NSDAP; and 20 April, Hitler's birthday.

Private family life was frequently disrupted when people were called upon to attend party camp (*lager*). Here, they were given a uniform, and fed propaganda. In their daily lives, Germans were encouraged to perform rituals to show their loyalty to the regime. The most famous was the Nazi salute, which involved raising the right arm at an angle and saying 'Heil Hitler'.

For those who opposed the government, there was the ever-present threat of the Gestapo. In every apartment block, a warden checked on people's movements, and reported anything suspicious to the police. Many of those who fell under suspicion were sent to concentration camps where they were frequently worked to death.

WOMEN

Hitler realized that he would need a large population to fight wars of conquest and settle the new lands to the east. Women were therefore encouraged to see themselves primarily as child-bearers and home-makers. Those who had at least four children were given a medal known as the *Mutterkreuz* (Mother's Cross) every year on Hitler's mother's birthday.

RIGHT *One of the many Nazi propaganda posters emphasizing the role of a woman as wife and mother.*

Women were also discouraged from taking up full-time work or doing training courses that might lead to professional careers. In 1933, all married women in the upper ranks of the civil service and medicine were dismissed, and women were excluded from jobs in law and politics. Laws were passed restricting the number of hours women could work in factories and banning them from certain jobs in heavy industry. The government also used loans and tax incentives to take women out of the workplace.

Partly as a result of these policies, the birth rate increased by almost 37 per cent between 1932 and 1937. However, towards the end of the 1930s, the increasing labour requirements of the Four-Year Plan forced the government to relax its rules. Even housewives with children were encouraged to work part-time, and increasingly women began entering professions such as medicine and teaching. By May 1939, 12.7 million women were in employment, making up 37 per cent of the workforce.

? PEOPLE IN QUESTION

Gertrud Scholtz-Klink (1902–99)

Scholtz-Klink, known as the lady Führer, was held up by the Nazis as a perfect example of German womanhood. Tall and blonde, she was married at 18 and had a total of 11 children by the time she was 32. Scholtz-Klink was appointed Reich Women's Leader in 1934. She was an ideal spokeswoman for the Nazis since she was convinced that a woman's place was in the home, bearing children and serving her husband. But how effective was Scholtz-Klink as an example to German womanhood? The evidence suggests that German women were generally as willing as men to believe in Nazi propaganda. Millions of women actively supported the Nazis, and were content to play the traditional role of wife and mother in the early 1930s. However, many were not taken in by Scholtz-Klink's rhetoric and some joined banned left-wing groups. In October 1933, the Nazis opened the first concentration camp for women at Moringen. By 1939, the growing number of women political prisoners caused them to open two more at Lichtenburg and Ravensbruck.

BELOW *Members of Nazi women's and students' clubs parading through the streets of Saarbrucken, western Germany, in 1935.*

ABOVE *A unit of the League of German Girls on the march. Girls were expected to run 60 metres in 14 seconds, throw a ball 12 metres, complete a 2-hour march, swim 100 metres, and know how to make a bed.*

CHILDREN

The Nazi leaders knew that young people were impressionable and full of energy that could be harnessed to the cause of national socialism. Children were used to report on the activities of their parents to the authorities. And young people were regularly exposed to Nazi ideology, both in the classroom and as members of Nazi youth organizations such as the Hitler Youth.

The Hitler Youth was set up in the 1920s, and by 1933 it had 108,000 members. In 1939, when membership was made compulsory, it had increased to nearly 9 million. The organization was divided into two branches, one for boys and one for girls. Boys aged 10 to 14 became members of the German Young Folk, before graduating to the Hitler Youth between 15 and 18. The equivalent groups for girls were the League of Young Girls and the League of German Girls.

The boys' groups tended to have a very military flavour, to prepare boys for their eventual role as soldiers. Their outings involved marching, pitching tents in perfect lines, singing military songs and engaging in mock battles. Girls would go camping and play organized sports. Both boys and girls had to attend regular lectures about national socialism. Girls were kept very busy, so they had little time for study, and were less likely to pursue a career.

ABOVE *A poster advertising the Hitler Youth. Despite such publicity, by 1938 attendance at Hitler Youth meetings was very poor – barely 25 per cent – and so a law was passed in 1939 making attendance compulsory.*

? EVENT IN QUESTION

How effective was the Hitler Youth?

On the face of it, the Hitler Youth appears to have been one of the most successful of all the Nazi organizations. During the 1930s, it grew into a genuine mass movement, giving young people a sense of belonging and a taste for healthy, outdoor activities. The writer Christa Wolff recalled her experiences in the Hitler Youth as offering her '*the promise of a loftier life*'. Albert Speer saw the hiking trips as a means of '*escaping the demands of a world growing increasingly complicated*'. However, the Nazis were more interested in creating a generation of loyal and aggressive followers than free-spirited nature-lovers. By the late 1930s, the organization had grown almost too successful. Its ageing leaders struggled to cope with the huge numbers of new members, many of whom were bored by the activities they were forced to take part in.

WORKERS

In 1933, German workers lost the protection of their trade unions when these were replaced by the government-controlled German Labour Front, which fixed their wages, and increased the powers of their employers to hire and fire. As the Nazi Party still relied heavily on workers in order to expand its industrial – and especially arms – production, they then needed to boost workers' morale and productivity.

Councils of Trust were set up in factories. Council of Trust representatives, elected by the workforce, could take employers to specially created courts for mistreating employees. However, very few cases were ever brought against employers. A more successful attempt to improve workers' conditions was called 'Beauty of Work'. This scheme, run by a leading Nazi, Albert Speer, persuaded employers to install modern lighting, swimming baths and canteens in their factories. By 1939, 67,000 firms were associated with the movement.

BELOW *Nazi propaganda often targeted workers. This 1932 election poster says 'Worker: elect the front soldier Hitler!'.*

ARBEITER

WÄHLT DEN FRONTSOLDATEN

HITLER!

'STRENGTH THROUGH JOY'

A workers' leisure organization was established by the German Labour Front called 'Strength Through Joy' (KDF). Its function was to keep workers happy, healthy and refreshed, and to offer them some relief from the tedium of their jobs. Concerts and plays were performed in factories, and discounts were offered to workers at sailing, skiing and golf clubs. Through KDF, workers were also given opportunities to go on holidays at reduced prices. Although German workers paid for all these benefits through compulsory deductions from their pay packets, KDF was of great propaganda value to the Nazi regime.

ABOVE *Hitler inspecting the new Volkswagen (or 'People's Car') in 1938. On Hitler's left is the car's designer, Dr Ferdinand Porsche. As many as 300,000 workers bought these cars using a credit scheme.*

Did the workers accept the new conditions?

The Nazis created full employment, and made some efforts to improve the conditions of workers. Indeed, in the late 1940s, many working people in Germany looked back on 1934 to 1939 as a relatively happy period in their lives. Yet there is plenty of evidence to show that the workers did not meekly accept the conditions imposed on them by the regime. Labour shortages in some industries, such as mining and construction, gave the workers a great deal of bargaining power. This meant that, even without union representation, they were able to force up wages, or move to better-paid jobs in other places. There were also increasing amounts of absenteeism, strikes and go-slows. The government put a stop to this in 1938 by introducing labour conscription in key industries. Those who persisted with strikes and other forms of industrial action were sent to brutal 'camps of education for work' run by the Gestapo.

RIGHT *A German couple harvesting apples in the 1930s, near Berlin. By 1939, 1.4 million farm workers had moved to the cities, causing a severe farm labour shortage.*

FARMERS

In their propaganda, the Nazis described farmers as 'responsible carriers of German society renewing its strength from blood and soil'. However, this vision clashed with Hitler's more urgent goals of national self-sufficiency and rearmament. The government needed farmers to be sufficiently productive to feed the workforce in Germany's growing industrial towns and cities.

To increase agricultural efficiency, all farmers were compelled to join the newly formed Reich Food Estate, which was responsible for all aspects of food production, including setting crop prices and future planning. The Reich Food Estate became very unpopular because it prevented farmers from charging higher prices despite food shortages in the cities. Agriculture remained poorly paid, and from 1934 farm workers began to migrate in large numbers to the cities.

Did the Nazis establish a new 'religion'?

Most Nazis distrusted Christianity, and a few dreamed of establishing a new state religion to replace it. One group founded a religion, called *Gottgläubig* ('God Believing'), based on pre-Christian pagan beliefs. However, this never became a mass movement. Another group planned to adapt the existing Christian faith to fit into Nazi ideology. They called this new religion 'Positive Christianity', and they preached that the Aryans were God's chosen race, and that inter-racial breeding was a sin. However, despite having the full powers of the state behind them, the Positive Christians never succeeded in imposing their beliefs on all German Christians. This was mainly due to the determined opposition of the Confessional Church.

RELIGION

The Nazis also wished to control Germany's churches. They set up a Reich Church to co-ordinate the country's 28 regional Protestant Churches. However, many of these Churches could not accept the racist views of the Nazi Protestants who dominated the Reich Church. Although most of the Churches outwardly co-operated with the regime, they also managed to retain some independence. One brave group of churchmen, led by Pastor Martin Niemöller of Dahlem, openly opposed the regime, and set up their own Confessional Church. When the Confessional Church continued to oppose the Nazis, the regime arrested several hundred of its leaders, including Niemöller.

The Catholic Church negotiated an agreement with the Nazis in July 1933. This guaranteed the Catholic Church freedom of worship and the right to administer itself. However, it lost all influence in politics with the abolition of its political party, the Centre Party, in 1933. It was also forced to accept the loss of its youth groups in 1939.

BELOW *Ludwig Muller, Reichsbishop of the German Evangelical Church, which was loyal to the Nazi regime.*

THE TREATMENT OF MINORITIES

Hitler wanted to create a Germany of 'racially pure', healthy people. To achieve this, Germany's ethnic minorities – the Jews, Gypsies, part-Africans and Slavs – would have to be removed. Furthermore, those Germans regarded as defective in some way, such as homosexuals, criminals and the mentally ill or physically disabled, would also need to be eliminated. During the 1930s, the Nazis started fulfilling these goals.

THE JEWS

BELOW *Women shoppers study a notice on a Jewish shop in April 1933, telling them to defend themselves against 'Jewish atrocity propaganda' and buy only from German retailers.*

In 1933, the Jewish community in Germany made up less than 1 per cent of the population, and most of them were fully integrated into German society. They were aware of Nazi anti-semitism, but had little idea of where it would eventually lead.

Not long after the Nazis came to power, they arranged a boycott of Jewish shops in April 1933. The same year, Jews were dismissed from their posts in the civil service, universities, medicine and journalism.

In September 1935, the notorious Nuremberg Laws were announced. These laws deprived Jews of their citizenship and prevented them from marrying non-Jews. Goebbels and another leading Nazi, Reinhard Heydrich, organized a programme to encourage Jews to emigrate.

When a German diplomat was assassinated in Paris by a Jewish student in 1938, it gave the Nazis an excuse to attack the Jewish community. Goebbels organized a widespread assault on Jewish shops and synagogues on 9 November, which became known as *Kristallnacht* ('Crystal Night') because of all the broken glass. In total, 7,500 Jewish shops and 400 synagogues were destroyed. Ninety-one Jews were killed, and around 20,000 were sent to concentration camps.

? EVENT IN QUESTION

Why didn't more German Jews emigrate?

During the 1930s, the Nazis made life progressively more difficult for Germany's 600,000 Jews. As a result, between 1933 and 1938, about 150,000 left Germany to begin new lives elsewhere. But why didn't more German Jews leave? Mainly because they could not find countries willing to take them. Around 100,000 European Jews were admitted to the USA before 1939; Britain accepted 80,000; and British-controlled Palestine took 70,000 by 1941. But these were just a tiny proportion of the approximately 11 million Jews under Nazi control by this time. Even after well-publicized events such as *Kristallnacht*, foreign countries remained reluctant to accept Jews. Some historians believe that this was because their governments were anti-semitic. Others have suggested that the Nazis only pretended to encourage emigration, and really wished to trap the Jews in Europe. By stripping Jews of their wealth, they made it impossible for them to travel, even if they had been admitted to other countries.

ETHNIC MINORITIES

Germany's other ethnic groups were very small in number. There were around 30,000 Sinti and Roma Gypsies; just 145 part-African children living in the Rhineland; and around 70,000 Sorbs of Slav descent. The part-African children were sterilized in 1937, to prevent any from having children later. When war broke out, the Gypsies were at first sent to work camps, and later many died in the gas chambers. After the invasion of Czechoslovakia in 1938–39, Sorb leaders, suspected of disloyalty, were placed in concentration camps.

BELOW *A German doctor checks the ethnic background of a Gipsy woman in 1940.*

CRIMINALS AND HOMOSEXUALS

The Nazis believed that people became criminals, alcoholics or tramps because of genetic defects. A law was passed in November

? **EVENT IN QUESTION**

Did doctors co-operate willingly with the killing of the disabled?

It is difficult today to understand how medically trained people could have voluntarily killed people with disabilities and diseases. In 1946, 26 doctors and public health officials were put on trial for their involvement in the euthanasia programme. They expressed no remorse, claiming that Germany faced a struggle for national survival, and that ordinary moral standards did not apply in such times. Some of the doctors justified their actions as 'mercy killings' for people with incurable illnesses. In fact the programme was based on the idea that vulnerable people have no right to care or even life.

1933, allowing the compulsory castration of serious criminals, to prevent them having children. In 1937, the Ministry of the Interior authorized the arrest of beggars and alcoholics with contagious diseases. Over the following year, more than 10,000 were imprisoned in concentration camps, where most of them died. Homosexuals, regarded as 'sexual deviants', were also persecuted. Between 1937 and 1939, around 15,000 were sent to concentration camps.

THE DISABLED AND MENTALLY ILL

The physically or mentally disabled – including those of German descent – were regarded as being of 'lesser racial value'. The Nazis believed that people with inherited diseases would 'pollute' the German gene pool. They argued that, to preserve the future health of the nation, it was necessary to adopt a policy of euthanasia. The Greek word euthanasia means 'an easy or merciful death'. To the Nazis, the term meant the elimination of 'lives not worth living'. In 1938, Hitler ordered that children with inherited deformities should be killed. In mid-1939, the programme was extended to include adults. By August 1941, when the programme was officially stopped, over 93,000 people had been killed. It continued in secret, and by the end of the war an estimated 275,000 had been killed, mostly in gas chambers.

CHAPTER 5

Nazi Germany at War, 1939–43

After his invasion and conquest of Poland in late 1939, Hitler turned his attention to western Europe. In April and May 1940, the Germans invaded Denmark, Norway, Holland, Belgium, Luxembourg and France. By June, most of western Europe was under German control, or neutral. Only Britain remained unconquered. The Battle of Britain, between the British and German airforces, took place from July to September 1940. Despite having more planes and men than the British RAF, the German *Luftwaffe* were unable to defeat them. It was Hitler's first setback in the war.

BELOW *Freezing German soldiers taken prisoner by the Russians during the retreat.*

In April 1941, German forces invaded Yugoslavia and Greece. Then, on 22 June, Hitler began his long-planned attack on the Soviet Union. After penetrating deep into Soviet territory, the German advance was halted outside Moscow in December. That month, America declared war on Germany's ally, Japan, and Hitler responded by declaring war on the USA.

By the winter of 1942, German fortunes were changing for the worse. On 11 November, German troops were defeated by the British in North Africa, and were forced to retreat. On 23 November, the German Sixth Army found itself surrounded by Russian forces at Stalingrad,

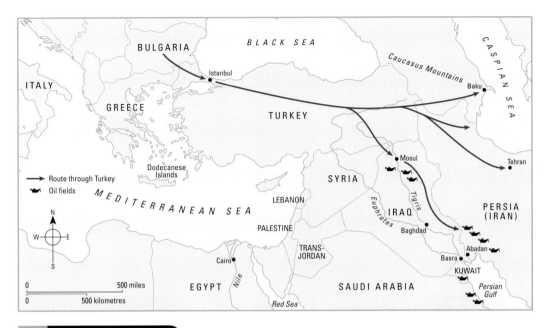

WHAT IF...

Hitler had not attacked the Soviet Union in June 1941?

Hitler's greatest military blunder was perhaps to attack the Soviet Union in the summer of 1941. By doing this, he exposed Germany to the dangers of a two-front war, with Britain still undefeated in Europe. Overthrowing the hated Soviet communist regime was a project close to Hitler's heart, and this may have clouded his judgement. Yet there were also practical reasons for the attack: Hitler wished to capture the Soviet Union's vast natural resources – particularly its oil. A better strategy at this stage might have been to invade neutral Turkey, followed by northern Iraq (with its large oil reserves), and from there to strike at Persia (now Iran), an even larger centre of oil production. German forces would then have been well placed to capture the Caspian Sea oil reserves on the Soviet Union's southern border. By mid-1942, the Germans could have launched attacks to the south and west of the Soviet Union, making a German victory far more likely.

ABOVE *A map showing the route Hitler's armies might have taken, had he opted for a southern attack on the Soviet Union, after capturing the oil fields in Iraq and Iran.*

leading to its final surrender on 31 January 1943. The following May, the German African army surrendered to British and American forces. Finally, in July, Benito Mussolini, Hitler's ally in Italy, was overthrown. Hitler's forces were now firmly on the defensive.

ABOVE *A group of Jews*
rounded up from the
Warsaw Ghetto wait to
go to the death camps.

THE HOLOCAUST

The German conquest of Poland brought between 2 and 3 million Jews under Nazi control. In 1940 and early 1941, many of the half a million Jews in western Europe were sent to live in run-down areas called ghettos. With the invasion of the Soviet Union in June 1941, some 3 million more Jews found themselves in Nazi-occupied territory.

At some point in mid-1941, Nazi policy towards the Jews changed. Instead of imprisoning captured Jews, the Nazis began killing them. SS taskforces followed the advancing German army into the Soviet Union. When they reached a village, they would round up the Jewish residents, march them into the countryside and shoot them. By spring 1942, over a million Jews had been murdered.

In January 1942, a conference of senior Nazi officials had been held at Wannsee, in Berlin. There it was decided that the exter-

? **EVENT IN QUESTION**

Did Hitler plan the Holocaust?

Did Hitler plan the mass murder of the Jews during the 1930s, or was it a policy that only emerged in 1941? Although Hitler always openly expressed his hatred of the Jews, he never stated clearly what he intended to do about it. Most of the anti-semitic policies of 1933–39 resulted from government ministers' interpretations of Hitler's views, rather than direct orders from the Führer. For instance, Hitler was careful not to associate himself with 'Crystal Night' (see page 36) in 1938, and there is no order bearing his signature to carry out the exterminations that began in 1941. However, in November 1938 he told Goering to 'solve' the Jewish question 'one way or another', and in January 1939 he informed the Reichstag that war would lead to the 'annihilation of the Jewish race in Europe'. Hitler may not have had precise plans for the Holocaust, but there is plenty of evidence to suggest that he intended it to happen.

ABOVE *Allied soldiers who entered the death camps when the war ended were often unprepared for the horrors they found there.*

mination of the Jews should be turned into a systematic operation. Death camps were built in Poland at Belzec, Sobibor, Majdanek, Chelmno and Auschwitz. Millions of Jews were transported to these camps from all over occupied Europe. Most were killed with poisonous gas in chambers disguised as shower rooms, and their bodies were then burned. Each camp was capable of killing 15,000 to 25,000 people per day.

The mass extermination of European Jews, known as the Holocaust, only stopped when the Nazis were defeated by the Allies in 1945. By then, between 5 and 6 million Jews had been killed.

RIGHT *A Nazi
propaganda poster
urging civilians to
support the war effort.
From January 1943 –
due to severe labour
shortages in the arms
factories – all non-
military men between
16 and 65, and all
women between 17 and
45, had to register for
'war work'.*

DER SIEG WIRD UNSER SEIN!

THE HOME FRONT

During the war years, Hitler became increasingly obsessed with military planning, leaving him with little time for domestic matters. Nevertheless, he would not permit the appointment of a home affairs committee, mainly because he feared that it might one day challenge his own authority. As a result, the Reich suffered from an absence of clear leadership during this period.

THE PARTY DURING THE WAR

The *Gauleiters* (or local party officials) were responsible for upholding public morale on the home front. The *Gauleiters* saw the Churches as their biggest rivals in this task, and they waged a fierce campaign against them. Christian magazines were banned, Catholic nuns were barred from carrying out welfare activities, and some members of the clergy were attacked and killed.

The party also used the war emergency to extend its control over children. Around 2 million children were moved to evacuation centres in the countryside in 1940. Officially this was to protect them from air raids, but it was also an opportunity to remove them from their families and schools and place them in the care of the Hitler Youth. The children received six hours of education each day, and spent much of the rest of their waking hours engaged in military-style activities.

In August 1942, Bormann, a senior Nazi, infiltrated the German justice system by getting one of his supporters appointed Minister of Justice. By doing so, he ensured that judges made their decisions in accordance with the party's wishes. After the German defeat at Stalingrad (see pages 40–41), the army also became increasingly dominated by the party. From July 1944 , the traditional military salute was replaced by the Nazi salute.

BELOW *Martin Bormann appeared very loyal to Hitler but when he realized that Germany would lose the war he tried to escape through the Russian lines. For some time, no one knew whether he was alive or dead. However his remains were found in Berlin in 1972.*

? PEOPLE IN QUESTION

Who had the greatest influence on Hitler during the war years?

The war was a time of power struggles within the Nazi leadership. Senior Nazis, such as Goebbels, Goering, Martin Bormann and Himmler, jostled for position. Usually the one with the most access to Hitler exercised the greatest power. In 1942, Bormann, who was head of the party, also became Hitler's personal secretary. In this position he controlled which papers Hitler saw, and was often able to prevent rivals from seeing Hitler, greatly increasing his influence over government policy. By advancing his own position, Bormann was also able to increase the influence of the party.

THE SS

By the start of the war, the SS was a massive organization that functioned almost like a mini-state. The prisoners in its network of concentration camps acted as a slave labour force, used exclusively in SS-controlled industries, such as mining, quarrying, food and arms production. The SS was the organization chiefly responsible for carrying out the Holocaust.

THE WAR ECONOMY

BELOW *An assembly line of the enormous underground V-2 rocket bomb plant at Nordhausen, Germany.*

Despite massive increases in military spending, German armaments firms were slow to introduce modern mass production techniques. There was also a labour shortage, with 6 million young men removed to the armed forces. By late 1941, the war

economy was in crisis. Hitler demanded increased efficiency in arms production. In February, Albert Speer was appointed Armaments Minister. He took control of weapons design away from the armed forces, and encouraged greater efficiency in weapons production. These reforms resulted in dramatic increases in production, which reached its peak in 1943–44, despite heavy Allied bombing.

RATIONING

For most of the war, the German population had enough food, and there was little hunger. However, the Allies prevented many goods from reaching Germany, and many resources were diverted to the war effort, so the standard of living for most Germans dropped considerably. A system of rationing was introduced, offering a diet 7–15 per cent above the minimum number of calories needed for health. Priority was given to soldiers' families and workers in the armaments industry.

? **PEOPLE IN QUESTION**

Albert Speer (1905–81)

Albert Speer was Hitler's chief architect, and a highly efficient Minister of Armaments from 1942 to 1945. As the only Nazi to plead guilty to war crimes at Nuremberg, he acquired the reputation of 'the good Nazi'. He served 20 years in jail, and wrote his memoirs in which he presented himself as a man who was guilty – not because he knew about the Holocaust, but because he should have known. Speer's biographer, Gitta Sereny, concluded that Speer was a man of excellent abilities, genuinely sorry that he had allowed himself to be associated with Hitler's crimes. Another historian, Dan van der Vat, takes a more negative view, claiming that a man of Speer's seniority must have known exactly what was going on in the death camps, and that his apologies were not genuine. Henry King, one of the prosecutors at Nuremberg, presents Speer as an essentially decent man, who was undone by ambition, but who partly redeemed himself at the end by defying Hitler's irrational order in 1945 to destroy the remains of German industry.

WOMEN

With so many men away fighting, women were conscripted in large numbers to work in factories, drive buses and trains, and even help with home defence duties. In addition, they had to look after their children and give support to their husbands on leave from the front. All these pressures caused tensions in many marriages.

WORKERS

Factory employees had to adapt to mass-production techniques, and get used to working alongside women and foreign workers. They also had to live with the constant threat of air raids. By 1944, overtime payments were abolished and the working week was increased to 60 hours. In spite of this, the workforce remained disciplined, mainly out of fear of being sent to the eastern front where the German army was suffering appalling casualty rates.

RIGHT *German city girls being shown how to pot plants in March 1940. Many were sent to farms to relieve the acute labour shortage in the countryside.*

❓ EVENT IN QUESTION

How effective was Allied bombing in lowering German morale?

Between 1942 and 1945, British and American planes repeatedly bombed the larger German cities. In May 1942, the centre of Cologne was engulfed in a firestorm that left only the cathedral standing. In July 1943, 30,000 people were killed in Hamburg in a four-night raid. Berlin was continually bombed from November 1943 until the end of the war. Worst-hit was Dresden, where 100,000 were killed in a single night. The planners of these air raids had hoped that they would break the morale of German citizens, and perhaps even provoke a popular uprising against the Nazis. In fact, German morale was actually strengthened by the bombing, and there was no large-scale movement to overthrow the regime. However, the bombing did indirectly affect civilian morale – firstly, by disrupting transport facilities and preventing vital products from reaching the shops; and secondly by forcing the authorities to evacuate the cities.

BELOW *A Berliner walks with his possessions to the city's railway station in 1948. Although badly damaged, the station continued to function through the war years and beyond.*

RURAL LIFE

During the war, food prices were strictly controlled, reducing farmers' incomes. Their horses were frequently taken by the regime to help with the war effort, and many young farm workers were conscripted into the armed forces or the factories, causing a labour shortage in the countryside.

In 1940, some 2 million children were evacuated from German cities. As the Allied bombing intensified in 1943 and 1944, a further 9 million women, children and elderly men were evacuated or escaped from the cities. Such a large migration caused tensions in the countryside. Although some evacuees did their fair share of work, others lived off their government allowances, and did little to help their rural hosts.

CHAPTER 6

Resistance to the Nazis

Many Germans hated the Nazis but, because of the SS and the Gestapo, it was dangerous to express their opposition. Some found secret ways of defying the regime, for example by hiding Jews, reading banned literature, listening to the BBC, or even refusing to give the 'Heil Hitler' salute. Others, such as some writers and intellectuals, withdrew from public life.

BELOW *Dr Martin Niemöller, President of the Confessional Church, who openly opposed the Nazis and spent seven years in a concentration camp.*

THE CHURCHES

The Catholic Church was largely silent on political issues, although it did fight in vain to prevent its youth groups being absorbed into the Hitler Youth. The Confessional Church remained independent of the Nazi-controlled Reich Church, and protested at the Nazi invasion of Czechoslovakia, but generally avoided direct confrontation with the regime. On issues where they had public support, the Churches sometimes spoke out more forcefully. For example, in August 1941 Bishop Galen of Munster publicly condemned the euthanasia programme (see page 39). Some brave churchmen, including nearly 400 priests who died at Buchen-wald concentration camp, actively opposed the Nazis.

LEFT-WING ORGANIZATIONS

The outlawed SPD established itself as an opposition party in exile in Prague, then Paris. However, it failed to set up an organized opposition within Germany itself. The KPD (German Communist Party) was more successful, maintaining communist cells in factories, despite frequent Gestapo raids. The

KPD generally followed instructions from the communist regime in Moscow, which in 1935 ordered them to combine their resources with the SPD.

YOUTH OPPOSITION

In the late 1930s, young working-class people in western Germany began rebelling against the highly disciplined environment of the Hitler Youth, forming gangs called 'Eidelweiss Pirates'. The Eidelweiss Pirates often attacked Hitler Youth patrols, and the more political ones distributed communist leaflets.

 EVENT IN QUESTION

Could the Catholic Church have done more to resist the Nazis?

The Catholic Church never publicly condemned the Nazis. Pope Pius XII did not even speak out when 8,000 Jews were arrested in Rome in 1943, and sent to the death camps. Why this silence? The Vatican (the Church leadership) approved of the Nazis' anti-communist policies, and may have regarded the Nazis as 'a lesser evil'. The Vatican has said that Pius XII dared not speak out for fear of endangering the lives of Jews and Catholics in Europe. However, this argument makes little sense, since the Nazis were planning to kill all the Jews anyway. In fact, if Pius had spoken out, it might have helped the Jews in Catholic countries by encouraging local bishops to resist the Nazis.

MILITARY AND CONSERVATIVE RESISTANCE

The greatest threat to Hitler's position came from a group of senior figures in Germany's army and civil service. On several occasions, these men came close to assassinating Hitler, or launching a military revolt.

The first plot came in summer 1938, when army officers became alarmed at Hitler's plans to trigger a European war. Six generals decided that, as soon as war was declared, they would have Hitler arrested, and declare martial law (emergency military rule). The plan was cancelled when a peace treaty was signed at Munich soon afterwards.

In 1941, a group known as the Kreisau Circle (an alliance of conservative, Christian and socialist opponents of the Nazi regime) was formed. At its core was the conservative aristocrat, Count Helmuth von Moltke. The group met frequently at Moltke's country house. It was exposed by the Gestapo in January 1944, and Moltke was later executed.

There were several assassination attempts on Hitler by military officers in 1943–44 but the one that came closest to succeeding was Operation Valkyrie, in July 1944. On 20 July, Colonel Claus von Stauffenberg attended one of Hitler's military briefings, placed a briefcase-bomb near where Hitler was sitting, and left to make a phone call. The bomb exploded, but Hitler was shielded from its full force by a table leg, and escaped with minor injuries. In the wake of this attempt, more than 5,000 suspected plotters were executed, and there was no further military or conservative resistance.

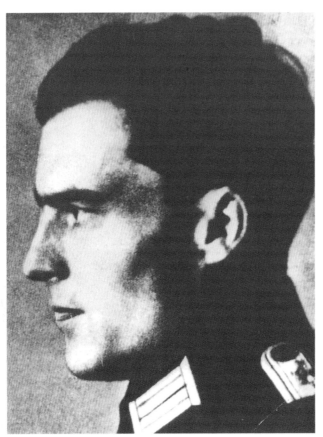

BELOW *Colonel Claus von Stauffenberg, who almost succeeded in killing Hitler. He was executed in Berlin a few hours after the failed assassination attempt.*

? WHAT IF...

a group of army officers had succeeded in assassinating Hitler?

From the notes left by members of the Kreisau Circle, and other opposition groups, it is possible to work out what might have occurred following a successful assassination of Hitler in, say, 1943. The new government would first have negotiated peace terms with the Allies. (Some opposition groups wished Germany to remain the dominant power in Europe, while others, such as the Kreisau Circle, saw Germany as just one country in a politically united Europe.) The coup leaders would probably then have drafted a new constitution. Few members of the conservative opposition wanted a return to democracy. Most favoured the restoration of the monarchy, or rule by a conservative elite. Whatever form the new government took, its main task would have been to stop the war and it would almost certainly have closed down the death camps, thus saving millions of lives.

BELOW: *Hitler and his Italian ally, Mussolini, inspect Hitler's wrecked headquarters after the bomb attack of July 1944. Hitler believed his survival was a miracle, and a sign that Germany would eventually win the war.*

CHAPTER 7

The End of Nazi Germany, 1944–45

ABOVE *Allied troops heading for Normandy in June 1944.*

MILITARY DEFEAT

After the defeat of German forces in North Africa and the Soviet Union (see pages 40–41), Hitler never regained the initiative in the war. In June 1944, the Allies invaded France. By August, Paris had been retaken and, by the end of September, Belgium and Holland had been liberated. Meanwhile, the Soviet army defeated the Germans and their allies in Poland, Romania and Bulgaria, and by January 1945 they were only 60 km (37 miles) east of Berlin.

As defeat loomed, Hitler retreated into a fantasy world. Despite all evidence to the contrary, he still believed he could win, pinning his hopes on the development of new missiles known as V-1 and V-2 rockets (see page 46), or a split between the Soviet Union and the USA. Hitler insisted that German forces should fight to the bitter end, leading to far greater losses than were necessary.

Early in 1945, following defeat in the Battle of the Bulge in occupied France, Hitler moved to Berlin to make his last stand against the advancing Allies. He never took responsibility for the devastation he had caused, but blamed the western powers and the Jews for causing the war, and his own generals for Germany's defeat.

ABOVE Crowds cheer as a French armoured column passes through the small French town of St Mère Eglise, in Normandy, June 1944.

Seeing no reason why Germany should survive him, he instructed Speer to destroy all German factories, power stations and public buildings. Fortunately, Speer managed to ignore this order. By the end of April, the Russians had almost taken Berlin, and Hitler, realizing the end was near, shot himself. The regime quickly collapsed, and on 10 May surrender terms were agreed with the Allies.

? WHAT IF...

Hitler had left military strategy to his generals?

By late 1943, Hitler's generals were struggling against the superior strength of the Allies, and he began to take control of strategy himself. But Hitler, who had only had very basic military training, was not a great strategist. His typical approach was to throw all his forces in one direction in the hope of achieving a devastating blow. The result invariably damaged the enemy but at great cost to his own forces. If Hitler had allowed his generals to make strategic decisions themselves, the war might have gone on longer, with more setbacks for the Allies. However, the eventual outcome would probably have been the same. The USA and Soviet Union had access to vastly greater resources, virtually assuring them of ultimate victory.

ABOVE *The ruins of Dresden following the Allied bombing raids on 13–15 February 1945. So intense was the bombing that it caused a firestorm similar to a tornado, powerful enough to pick people up and suck them into the flames.*

HOME FRONT

Intensive Allied bombing between 1942 and 1944 devastated German cities. Oil supplies fell to dangerously low levels, communications were severely disrupted, and food shortages became acute. By April 1945, the industrial areas of Silesia and the Ruhr were under Allied control, and the German war economy was no longer functioning.

Nevertheless, the Nazi regime retained its political grip on the nation right until the end. Himmler's Gestapo dealt ruthlessly with any signs of opposition. Most Germans, however, were less concerned with political rebellion than day-to-day survival. Shortages of rationed goods, such as butter, meat, textiles, coal and cigarettes, led to a growing black market (illegal trade).

Why did the Anglo-American forces not take Berlin?

During the Cold War (the 45-year conflict between the West and the Soviet Union that followed the Second World War) the question was often asked: why did the British and American forces not capture Berlin? This would have brought the city within Western control, instead of leaving it as a divided city – its pro-Western half isolated within the communist east for over four decades. On 11 April 1945, the American forces came within 96 km (60 miles) of Berlin. There were no German defences left outside the capital but they did not attack. Why? Firstly, General Eisenhower, commander of the US forces, decided that it would be too costly in lives (he estimated it could lead to around 250,000 casualties), and he preferred to leave it to the Russians. Secondly, the Soviet and American political leaders had decided earlier that Berlin fell within the 'Soviet zone of occupation'. And finally, the Allies wrongly believed that Hitler would make his last stand not in Berlin but in a network of caves in the southern German Alps.

In mid-1944 Goebbels developed a plan for 'total mobilization', designed to focus the whole nation's energies on the war. A 'People's Army' of very old and very young men, including any aged between 16 and 65 who were not already serving the country, was cobbled together to make a last-ditch stand against the invading forces.

By early 1945, the Nazi Party itself was disintegrating. Many *Gauleiters* had exploited their position during the war, in order to live well, while the rest of the population suffered. They used brutal methods to impose order, ranging from harassment to murder. As defeat loomed, they tried to save themselves by blending into the civilian population.

BELOW *Hitler awards an Iron Cross to a 12-year-old Hitler Youth soldier in 1945 as the Russians close in on Berlin. This is one of the last photographs of the Nazi leader to have survived.*

LEGACY

The Nazi regime provoked a world war that caused the deaths of around 30 million soldiers and civilians. The Nazis also deliberately exterminated millions of Jews, and hundreds of thousands of Gypsies, Slavs, homosexuals, and the mentally ill. In Germany alone, 4.2 million people died in the war. Millions more were left injured, bereaved and homeless. Their country was in ruins – its cities bombed, and its territory occupied and partitioned by the victorious Allies. For 45 years – until its reunification in 1990 – Germany was split into two separate countries, commonly known as East Germany (Russian-controlled) and West Germany.

THE NUREMBERG WAR CRIMES TRIBUNAL

In 1946, 21 Nazi leaders stood trial for their crimes at Nuremberg. Almost all pleaded not guilty, claiming ignorance, or

BELOW Nazi leaders on trial at Nuremberg in 1946. Hermann Goering can be seen seated in the front row with his chin in his hand. He avoided execution by swallowing poison on 15 October 1946.

EVENT IN QUESTION

Was denazification successful?

The victorious powers were determined to root out and destroy any remaining elements of national socialism. Between 1945 and 1950, they carried out a programme known as 'denazification', which involved trying people for war crimes, and re-educating the German people to counteract the effects of 12 years of Nazi propaganda. However, many Germans who lived through the Nazi era generally preferred to get on with their lives and not face up to the crimes of national socialism. It was left to a younger generation, growing up in the 1960s, to ask questions about the Nazi regime and their parents' involvement in it.

that they were merely following orders. Another popular defence was that terrible things happen in wartime, and that other countries were guilty too.

THE ECONOMIC MIRACLE

In the 1950s and 1960s, West Germany experienced massive industrial growth, making it the world's fourth largest economy. However, this 'economic miracle' would not have been possible without the 1930s rearmament programme. (Despite Allied bombing, this programme left the West Germans with many factories well-equipped for mass-production.) The German Labour Front – another Nazi legacy – contributed to better relations between management and workforce in the post-war era.

LESSONS FOR THE FUTURE

The history of Nazi Germany shows how easy it is for a nation to fall prey to violent, hate-filled, anti-democratic forces. Today, people are as vulnerable as ever to political movements that – like the Nazis – appeal to the basest human instincts, such as fear and hatred of those who appear different. People all over the world need to be on their guard against the re-emergence of racism and prejudice, and ensure that what happened in Germany in the 1930s and 1940s never happens again.

Timeline

1919
JANUARY: German Workers' Party (DAP) is founded in Munich.

1920
FEBRUARY: DAP changes its name to the National Socialist German Workers' Party (NSDAP).

1921
JULY: Hitler becomes leader of the NSDAP.
AUGUST: SA is formed.

1923
NOVEMBER: Munich Beerhall Coup.
NSDAP is banned.

1924
APRIL: Hitler is given a five-year prison sentence.
DECEMBER: Hitler is released from prison.

1925
FEBRUARY: Nazi Party is re-founded.

1928
MAY: Nazis fight their first election, and win 12 seats in the Reichstag.

1930
SEPTEMBER: Nazis win 107 seats in the Reichstag.

1932
APRIL: Hitler stands in presidential elections and loses to Hindenburg.
JULY: Nazis become the largest party in the Reichstag with 230 seats.
NOVEMBER: Nazis win 196 seats in the Reichstag.

1933
JANUARY: Hitler is appointed Chancellor.
FEBRUARY: Reichstag fire.
MARCH: Enabling Act is passed.
APRIL: Boycott of Jewish businesses.
JULY: NSDAP is declared the only legal political party.

Concordat with the Catholic Church is signed.
NOVEMBER: Gestapo is set up.

1934
JUNE: 'Night of the Long Knives' – the purge of the SA.
JULY: SS becomes an independent organization.
AUGUST: Hindenburg dies. Hitler combines the roles of president and chancellor.

1935
MARCH: Military conscription reintroduced.
JULY: Reich Church set up to co-ordinate Germany's Protestant Churches.
SEPTEMBER: Nuremberg Race Laws announced.

1936
MARCH: Remilitarization of Rhineland.
APRIL: Goering appointed Commissioner of Raw Materials.
JUNE: Himmler appointed Head of the German Police.

OCTOBER: The Four-Year Plan is announced.

1938

MARCH: Annexation of Austria.

OCTOBER: Occupation of Sudetenland.

DECEMBER: *Kristallnacht* ('Crystal Night').

1939

MARCH: Membership of Hitler Youth becomes compulsory for all children aged between 10 and 18.

AUGUST: Food rationing is introduced.

SEPTEMBER: German invasion of Poland.

1940

APRIL: German invasion of Denmark and Norway.

MAY: German invasion of Holland, Belgium,

Luxembourg and France begins.

JUNE: France surrenders.

JULY–SEPTEMBER: Battle of Britain.

1941

FEBRUARY: German troops sent to North Africa.

JUNE: German invasion of the Soviet Union.

DECEMBER: Germany and Italy declare war on the USA.

1942

JANUARY: Wannsee Conference.

MARCH: The first Jews are sent from western Europe to be killed at Auschwitz.

OCTOBER: German and Italian troops are defeated in North Africa.

1943

JANUARY: German Sixth Army surrenders at Stalingrad.

MAY: German and Italian troops surrender in North Africa.

1944

JANUARY: Gestapo smashes opposition group, the Kreisau Circle.

JULY: Assassination attempt on Hitler fails.

OCTOBER: Germans slaughtered by Russian army.

1945

APRIL: Hitler commits suicide.

MAY: Germany surrenders.

Glossary

Allies The coalition of countries ranged against Nazi Germany and its allies in the Second World War, including the USA, Britain and the Soviet Union.

anti-semitism Prejudice against Jews.

Aryan In Nazi ideology, a white person who is regarded as racially superior.

boycott A refusal to deal with a business or businesses as a protest against it.

cell A small secret group of people who are part of a larger, political organization.

censor To check a letter or any form of publication and remove or change any part of it which is considered a threat to security.

Centre Party A political party set up in 1870 to represent the interests of Catholic Germans.

communist A person or group who believes in a system in which the state controls property, trade and production.

concentration camp A prison camp used for political prisoners or civilians.

Confessional Church A Church set up by a group of Protestants in 1934 in opposition to the Nazi-controlled Reich Church.

conscription Compulsory service, usually in the armed forces.

conservative Someone who believes in keeping things as they are, and preserving traditional ways of life and behaviour.

constitution A written document outlining the basic laws by which a country is governed.

coup The sudden overthrow of a government and seizure of political power.

demilitarized zone An officially recognized area from which all soldiers and weapons have been removed after an agreement.

democratic Allowing free and equal participation in government.

economic depression Period when trade is very poor, marked by unemployment and poverty.

ethnic group A group of a certain race, or a group that shares the same customs and culture.

ethnic minority A minority group with a similar cultural background.

extremist A person or group who holds extreme political or religious beliefs.

Gauleiter A regional Nazi party leader, in charge of a *Gau* (a division of the NSDAP) who controlled local party organizations.

gene pool The genes carried by all individuals in an interbreeding population.

genetic Relating to genes. A gene is the basic unit contained in the cells of all living things, which can transmit characteristics from one generation to the next.

Gestapo A shortened version of *Geheime Staatspolizei*, the secret state police in Nazi Germany.

ghetto A run-down area of a city lived in by a minority group.

ideology A system of beliefs that forms the basis of a social, economic or political philosophy.

inflation An increase in the supply of currency compared to the availability of goods, resulting in higher prices.

left-wing Supporting the idea of political or social change and reform.

lower middle class A section of society consisting of people with incomes a little higher than manual labourers, such as shopkeepers and owners of small businesses.

martial law The controlling of a civilian population by military forces and according to military rules.

mobilization The assembling and preparation of troops for war duty.

national socialism The ideology of the Nazi Party, which included national expansion, racism, and total control of the state and the economy.

nationalist A person or group who is loyal and devoted to a nation; sometimes this can also refer to a belief that a nation is better than other nations and has the right to dominate them.

Nationalist Party A right-wing German party.

NSDAP The National Socialist German Workers' Party, more familiarly known as the Nazi Party. The party acquired this name in February 1920, after being known as the German Workers' Party.

Further information

parliamentary democracy A system of government in which representatives are elected by the people to govern by passing laws through a parliament.

patriot Somebody who proudly supports or defends his or her country.

personality cult Officially encouraged worship of a leader.

propaganda Organized publicity, often by a government, to promote a particular view.

purge The removal of political opponents.

Reich The German state. The First Reich was the Holy Roman Empire (926–1806) and the Second Reich was the German Empire (1871–1919). The Nazi state is known as the Third Reich.

Reichstag The German parliament.

reparations Compensation demanded from a defeated nation by a victorious nation in a war.

republic A political system in which the ruler is an elected president rather than a monarch.

right-wing Supporting the idea of maintaining social and political systems as they are.

SA A short form of *Sturmabteilung* or storm troops, a street army set up by the Nazis in 1921, used to protect party meetings and attack their enemies.

socialist A person who believes in a system in which wealth is shared more equally, and industries and trade are controlled by the government.

Soviet Union Also known as the USSR (Union of Soviet Socialist Republics), a country formed from the territories of the Russian Empire in 1917, which lasted until 1991.

SPD The German Social Democratic Party, a socialist party and a major force in German politics between 1919 and 1933.

SS *Schutzstaffel* literally means 'Protection Squad', and the SS were set up in 1925 to protect leading Nazis.

supply lines The routes between the front line of an army, and its resources, such as food, ammunition and weaponry.

volkisch The term literally means 'folkish', but there is no direct English equivalent. It is used to describe a racist, anti-semitic ideology.

BOOKS

Elsbeth Emmerich, *My Childhood in Nazi Germany* (Hodder Wayland, 1991)

Charles Freeman, *New Perspectives: The Rise of the Nazis* (Hodder Wayland, 2001)

Liz Gogerly, *Twentieth-Century History Makers: Adolf Hitler* (Watts, 2002)

Jane Shuter, *The Holocaust: Prelude to the Holocaust* (Heinemann Library, 2002)

Richard Tames, *Ideas of the Modern World: Fascism* (Hodder Wayland, 2000)

PLACES TO VISIT

Imperial War Museum
Lambeth Road, London SE1 6HZ
Tel: 0207 416 5000

The Holocaust Centre, Beth Shalom,
Laxton, Newark, Notts, NG22 0PA
Tel: 01623 836627 Fax: 01623 836647

NOTE ON SOURCES

A source is information about the past. Sources can take many forms, from books, films and documents to physical objects and sound recordings.

There are two types of source, primary and secondary. Primary sources date from around the time you are studying; secondary sources, such as books like this, have been produced since that time.

Here are some guidelines to bear in mind when approaching a written or drawn primary source:

1. Who produced it (a politician, cartoonist, etc?) and why? What was their motive?
2. When exactly was the source produced?
3. Might the source have been altered by an editor, censor or translator?
4. Where was the source produced? Which country, town, region, etc?
5. Does the source tie in with other sources you have met, or does it offer a new point of view?
6. Where has the source come from? Has it been selected by someone else or did you find it through your own research?

Index